# THE SWiFT GaZeLLe CaN RUN QUiTe WeLL

## GRaSSLaND aNiMaLS

By MARK OBLINGER

Illustrated by RYAN WHEATCROFT

CANTATA
LEARNING

MANKATO, MINNESOTA

WWW.CANTATALEARNING.COM

**CANTATA**
**LEARNING**
MANKATO, MINNESOTA

Published by Cantata Learning
1710 Roe Crest Drive
North Mankato, MN 56003
www.cantatalearning.com

Library of Congress Control Number: 2014956987
978-1-63290-253-5 (hardcover/CD)
978-1-63290-405-8 (paperback/CD)
978-1-63290-447-8 (paperback)

*The Swift Gazelle Can Run Quite Well: Grassland Animals* by Mark Oblinger
Illustrated by Ryan Wheatcroft

Book design, Tim Palin Creative
Editorial direction, Flat Sole Studio
Executive musical production and direction, Elizabeth Draper
Music arranged and produced by Mark Oblinger

Printed in the United States of America.

VISIT
**WWW.CANTATALEARNING.COM/ACCESS-OUR-MUSIC**
TO SING ALONG TO THE SONG

Grasslands are covered in grasses. There are not many trees or shrubs. Grassland climates are hot, at least in the summer, and somewhat dry. Almost half of Africa is grasslands. North American prairies are grasslands too.

Now turn the page, and sing along.

Grasslands have few trees and brush to hide their many **creatures**.

Some animals run in groups as one. Let's learn about their **features**.

Zebra stripes are black and white.
Each one's different from the start.

But when they're running in a herd,
you can't tell them apart.

Lions are big cats that like to nap and dream of catching dinner.

They will feast on wildebeest.

Their **pride** makes them a winner.

Grasslands have few trees and brush
to hide their many creatures.

Some animals run in groups as one.
Let's learn about their features.

The swift gazelle can run quite well.

To speed, it's no stranger.

This antelope can sprint up **slopes**

and bound away from danger.

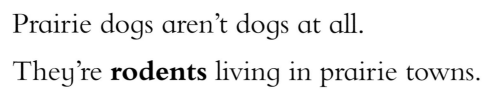

Prairie dogs aren't dogs at all.

They're **rodents** living in prairie towns.

When danger's near, they chirp to say,

"Everyone, quick, get underground!"

Kangaroos cruise on big back legs
that they use to hop and **crouch**.

Their babies get a cozy ride
inside their mother's **pouch**.

Grasslands have few trees and brush
to hide their many creatures.

Some animals run in groups as one.
Let's learn about their features.

# SONG LYRICS
## The Swift Gazelle Can Run Quite Well: Grassland Animals

Grasslands have few trees and brush
to hide their many creatures.

Some animals run in groups as one.
Let's learn about their features.

Zebra stripes are black and white.
Each one's different from the start.

But when they're running in a herd,
you can't tell them apart.

Lions are big cats that like to nap
and dream of catching dinner.

They will feast on wildebeest.
Their pride makes them a winner.

Grasslands have few trees and brush
to hide their many creatures.

Some animals run in groups as one.
Let's learn about their features.

The swift gazelle can run quite well.
To speed, it's no stranger.

This antelope can sprint up slopes
and bound away from danger.

Prairie dogs aren't dogs at all.
They're rodents living in prairie towns.

When danger's near, they chirp to say,
"Everyone, quick, get underground!"

Kangaroos cruise on big back legs
that they use to hop and crouch.

Their babies get a cozy ride
inside their mother's pouch.

Grasslands have few trees and brush
to hide their many creatures.

Some animals run in groups as one.
Let's learn about their features.

# The Swift Gazelle Can Run Quite Well: Grassland Animals

**World**
Mark Oblinger

**Chorus**

Grass - lands have few trees and brush to hide their man - y crea - tures. Some

an - i - mals run in groups as one. Let's learn a - bout their fea - tures.

**Verse**

1. Ze - bra stripes are black and white. Each one's dif - fer - ent from the start.

But when they're run - ning in a herd, you can't tell them a - part.

**Verse 2**

Lions are big cats that like to nap
and dream of catching dinner.
They will feast on wildebeest.
Their pride makes them a winner.

**Verse 3**

The swift gazelle can run quite well.
To speed, it's no stranger.
This antelope can sprint up slopes
and bound away from danger.

**Verse 4**

Prairie dogs aren't dogs at all.
They're rodents living in prairie towns.
When danger's near, they chirp to say,
"Everyone, quick, get underground!"

**Chorus**

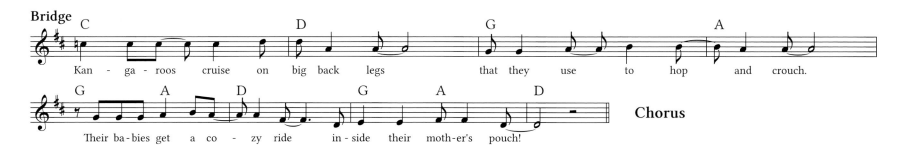

**Bridge**

Kan - ga - roos cruise on big back legs that they use to hop and crouch.

Their ba - bies get a co - zy ride in - side their moth-er's pouch!

**Chorus**

# GLOSSARY

**crouch**—to bend low

**creatures**—living beings

**features**—important facts about something

**pouch**—a flap of skin that looks like a pocket in which some animals carry their young

**pride**—a group of lions; pride also is the feeling of being proud

**rodents**—animals, such as mice, prairie dogs, and beavers, that have sharp front teeth for gnawing

**slopes**—surfaces with one end higher than the other

# GUIDED READING ACTIVITIES

1. What is a grassland?

2. Do any grassland animals live near you? Which ones?

3. Draw a picture of a grassland. Which plants and animals did you include?

## TO LEARN MORE

Callery, Sean. *Grassland*. New York: Kingfisher, 2011.

Kalman, Bobbie. *Baby Animals in Grassland Habitats*. New York: Crabtree, 2011.

Silverman, Buffy. *Grassland Food Chains*. Chicago: Heinemann Library, 2011.

Underwood, Deborah. *Hiding in Grasslands*. Chicago: Heinemann Library, 2011.